2019
Vocal Practice Journal

Name _____

If Found, Please Call:_____

E-mail: _____

Goals

My 5-year musical goals are: (be as specific as possible):

1._____
2._____
3._____
4._____
5._____

My 3-year musical goals are:

1._____
2._____
3._____
4._____
5._____

My 1-year musical goals are:

1._____
2._____
3._____
4._____
5._____

My goals for January-March are (complete before 1/1/19):

1._____
2._____
3._____
4._____
5._____

My goals for April-June are (complete before 4/1/19):

1._____
2._____
3._____
4._____
5._____

My goals for June-August are (complete before 6/1/19):

1._____
2._____
3._____
4._____
5._____

My goals for September-December are (complete before 9/1/19):

1._____
2._____
3._____
4._____
5._____

Repertoire

Repertoire Studied

1._____
2._____
3._____
4._____
5._____
6._____

Technical Studies

1._____
2._____
3._____
4._____
5._____
6._____

Repertoire I'd like to learn:

1._____
2._____
3._____
4._____
5._____
6._____

Public Performances:

Date   Performance Name   Location

1._____

2._____

3._____

4._____

5._____

6._____

7._____

8._____

9._____

10._____

Notes, questions, telephone numbers

Sample Week	Assignments for this week	Monday	Tuesday	Wednesday	Thursday
Warm-ups and exercises	1."ee" slides do-sol-do 2. ha do-mi-sol-mi-do x3 3. lip buzzes 4. "zee-ah" do-sol-fa-mi-re-	1.-4. 8:00-8:10	7:30-7:35	8:00-8:10	7:30-7:35
Repertoire	1.Lied der Mignon 2.Lydia 3.Shenandoah 4.Sebben crudele 5. Deh vieni non tardar	1. 8:10-8:40 Pitches and Rhythms	1. 7:35-7:40 Review 2. 7:40-8:20 Pitches and Rhythms	2. 8:10-8:15 Review 3. 8:15-8:30 Pitches and Rhythms 4. 8:30-8:55 Pitches and Rhythms	5. 7:35-7:55 Pitches and Rhythms 3. 7:55-8:10 Review 4. 8:10-8:20
Text Work	1.B-section on lied 2.2nd verse on on Lydia 3. Syncopation on Sebben 4.Translations on foreign language pieces	1. 10:00-10:15 Text on rhythm		3. 10:00-10:15 Text on Rhythm	4. 10:00-10:15 Text translation
Character/ Style Study	1.Plot+Character of aria 2. Ornaments (Sebben) 3. Faust History 4. French Melodie		3. 3:00-3:10 Research	2. 3:00-3:10 Research	
Listening	1.Listen t o 3 Faure songs 2.Listen to 3 versions of aria 3.Listen to Gretchen 4.Listen to other versions of Shenandoah	3. 10:15-10:20	1. 3:10-3:20		
Totals		1:00	1:10	1:20	1:05

Sample Week	Friday	Saturday	Sunday	Totals	Questions
Warm-ups and exercises	Day off	9:00-9:10	10:00-10:10	:50	
Repertoire		1-3. 9:10-9:55 Sing Through	4-5. 10:10-10:55 Sing Through	4:15	Double check pitches of aria recitative
Text Work		2. 10:00-10:15 Text on rhythm		1:00	How do I pronounce "schwindelt" Help with text rhythm in Lydia
Character/ Style Study			1. 2:00-2:15 Research	:35	How complicated do ornaments need to be?
Listening		4. 10:15-10:20	2. 2:15-2:30	:40	How much leniency is there in a folk song?
	0:00	1:20	1:25	7:20	

December 31, 2018	Assignments for this week	Monday	Tuesday	Wednesday	Thursday
Warm-ups and exercises	1. 2. 3. 4.				
Repertoire	1. 2. 3. 4.				
Text Work	1. 2. 3. 4.				
Character/ Style Study	1. 2. 3. 4.				
Listening	1. 2. 3. 4.				
Totals					

January 4, 2019	Friday	Saturday	Sunday	Totals	Questions
Warm-ups and exercises					
Repertoire					
Text Work					
Character/ Style Study					
Listening					

January 7, 2019	Assignments for this week	Monday	Tuesday	Wednesday	Thursday
Warm-ups and exercises	1. 2. 3. 4.				
Repertoire	1. 2. 3. 4.				
Text Work	1. 2. 3. 4.				
Character/ Style Study	1. 2. 3. 4.				
Listening	1. 2. 3. 4.				
Totals					

January 11, 2019	Friday	Saturday	Sunday	Totals	Questions
Warm-ups and exercises					
Repertoire					
Text Work					
Character/ Style Study					
Listening					

January 14, 2019	Assignments for this week	Monday	Tuesday	Wednesday	Thursday
Warm-ups and exercises	1. 2. 3. 4.				
Repertoire	1. 2. 3. 4.				
Text Work	1. 2. 3. 4.				
Character/ Style Study	1. 2. 3. 4.				
Listening	1. 2. 3. 4.				
Totals					

January 18, 2019	Friday	Saturday	Sunday	Totals	Questions
Warm-ups and exercises					
Repertoire					
Text Work					
Character/ Style Study					
Listening					

January 21, 2019	Assignments for this week	Monday	Tuesday	Wednesday	Thursday
Warm-ups and exercises	1. 2. 3. 4.				
Repertoire	1. 2. 3. 4.				
Text Work	1. 2. 3. 4.				
Character /Style Study	1. 2. 3. 4.				
Listening	1. 2. 3. 4.				
Totals					

January 25, 2019	Friday	Saturday	Sunday	Totals	Questions
Warm-ups and exercises					
Repertoire					
Text Work					
Character/ Style Study					
Listening					

January 28, 2019	Assignments for this week	Monday	Tuesday	Wednesday	Thursday
Warm-ups and exercises	1. 2. 3. 4.				
Repertoire	1. 2. 3. 4.				
Text Work	1. 2. 3. 4.				
Character/ Style Study	1. 2. 3. 4.				
Listening	1. 2. 3. 4.				
Totals					

February 1, 2019	Friday	Saturday	Sunday	Totals	Questions
Warm-ups and exercises					
Repertoire					
Text Work					
Character/ Style Study					
Listening					

February 4, 2019	Assignments for this week	Monday	Tuesday	Wednesday	Thursday
Warm-ups and exercises	1. 2. 3. 4.				
Repertoire	1. 2. 3. 4.				
Text Work	1. 2. 3. 4.				
Character/ Style Study	1. 2. 3. 4.				
Listening	1. 2. 3. 4.				
Totals					

February 8, 2019	Friday	Saturday	Sunday	Totals	Questions
Warm-ups and exercises					
Repertoire					
Text Work					
Character/ Style Study					
Listening					

February 11, 2019	Assignments for this week	Monday	Tuesday	Wednesday	Thursday
Warm-ups and exercises	1. 2. 3. 4.				
Repertoire	1. 2. 3. 4.				
Text Work	1. 2. 3. 4.				
Character/ Style Study	1. 2. 3. 4.				
Listening	1. 2. 3. 4.				
Totals					

February 15, 2019	Friday	Saturday	Sunday	Totals	Questions
Warm-ups and exercises					
Repertoire					
Text Work					
Character/ Style Study					
Listening					

February 18, 2019	Assignments for this week	Monday	Tuesday	Wednesday	Thursday
Warm-ups and exercises	1. 2. 3. 4.				
Repertoire	1. 2. 3. 4.				
Text Work	1. 2. 3. 4.				
Character/ Style Study	1. 2. 3. 4.				
Listening	1. 2. 3. 4.				
Totals					

February 22, 2019	Friday	Saturday	Sunday	Totals	Questions
Warm-ups and exercises					
Repertoire					
Text Work					
Character/ Style Study					
Listening					

February 25, 2019	Assignments for this week	Monday	Tuesday	Wednesday	Thursday
Warm-ups and exercises	1. 2. 3. 4.				
Repertoire	1. 2. 3. 4.				
Text Work	1. 2. 3. 4.				
Character/ Style Study	1. 2. 3. 4.				
Listening	1. 2. 3. 4.				
Totals					

March 1, 2019	Friday	Saturday	Sunday	Totals	Questions
Warm-ups and exercises					
Repertoire					
Text Work					
Character/ Style Study					
Listening					

March 4, 2019	Assignments for this week	Monday	Tuesday	Wednesday	Thursday
Warm-ups and exercises	1. 2. 3. 4.				
Repertoire	1. 2. 3. 4.				
Text Work	1. 2. 3. 4.				
Character/ Style Study	1. 2. 3. 4.				
Listening	1. 2. 3. 4.				
Totals					

Month to date total:_____

Year to date total_____

March 8, 2019	Friday	Saturday	Sunday	Totals	Questions
Warm-ups and exercises					
Repertoire					
Text Work					
Character/ Style Study					
Listening					

March 11, 2019	Assignments for this week	Monday	Tuesday	Wednesday	Thursday
Warm-ups and exercises	1. 2. 3. 4.				
Repertoire	1. 2. 3. 4.				
Text Work	1. 2. 3. 4.				
Character/ Style Study	1. 2. 3. 4.				
Listening	1. 2. 3. 4.				
Totals					

March 15, 2019	Friday	Saturday	Sunday	Totals	Questions
Warm-ups and exercises					
Repertoire					
Text Work					
Character/ Style Study					
Listening					

March 18, 2019	Assignments for this week	Monday	Tuesday	Wednesday	Thursday
Warm-ups and exercises	1. 2. 3. 4.				
Repertoire	1. 2. 3. 4.				
Text Work	1. 2. 3. 4.				
Character/ Style Study	1. 2. 3. 4.				
Listening	1. 2. 3. 4.				
Totals					

March 22, 2019	Friday	Saturday	Sunday	Totals	Questions
Warm-ups and exercises					
Repertoire					
Text Work					
Character/ Style Study					
Listening					

March 25, 2019	Assignments for this week	Monday	Tuesday	Wednesday	Thursday
Warm-ups and exercises	1. 2. 3. 4.				
Repertoire	1. 2. 3. 4.				
Text Work	1. 2. 3. 4.				
Character/ Style Study	1. 2. 3. 4.				
Listening	1. 2. 3. 4.				
Totals					

March 29, 2019	Friday	Saturday	Sunday	Totals	Questions
Warm-ups and exercises					
Repertoire					
Text Work					
Character/ Style Study					
Listening					

April 1, 2019	Assignments for this week	Monday	Tuesday	Wednesday	Thursday
Warm-ups and exercises	1. 2. 3. 4.				
Repertoire	1. 2. 3. 4.				
Text Work	1. 2. 3. 4.				
Character/ Style Study	1. 2. 3. 4.				
Listening	1. 2. 3. 4.				
Totals					

April 5, 2019	Friday	Saturday	Sunday	Totals	Questions
Warm-ups and exercises					
Repertoire					
Text Work					
Character/ Style Study					
Listening					

April 8, 2019	Assignments for this week	Monday	Tuesday	Wednesday	Thursday
Warm-ups and exercises	1. 2. 3. 4.				
Repertoire	1. 2. 3. 4.				
Text Work	1. 2. 3. 4.				
Character/ Style Study	1. 2. 3. 4.				
Listening	1. 2. 3. 4.				
Totals					

April 12, 2019	Friday	Saturday	Sunday	Totals	Questions
Warm-ups and exercises					
Repertoire					
Text Work					
Character/ Style Study					
Listening					

April 15, 2019	Assignments for this week	Monday	Tuesday	Wednesday	Thursday
Warm-ups and exercises	1. 2. 3. 4.				
Repertoire	1. 2. 3. 4.				
Text Work	1. 2. 3. 4.				
Character/ Style Study	1. 2. 3. 4.				
Listening	1. 2. 3. 4.				
Totals					

April 19, 2019	Friday	Saturday	Sunday	Totals	Questions
Warm-ups and exercises					
Repertoire					
Text Work					
Character/ Style Study					
Listening					

April 22, 2019	Assignments for this week	Monday	Tuesday	Wednesday	Thursday
Warm-ups and exercises	1. 2. 3. 4.				
Repertoire	1. 2. 3. 4.				
Text Work	1. 2. 3. 4.				
Character/ Style Study	1. 2. 3. 4.				
Listening	1. 2. 3. 4.				
Totals					

April 26, 2019	Friday	Saturday	Sunday	Totals	Questions
Warm-ups and exercises					
Repertoire					
Text Work					
Character/ Style Study					
Listening					

April 29, 2019	Assignments for this week	Monday	Tuesday	Wednesday	Thursday
Warm-ups and exercises	1. 2. 3. 4.				
Repertoire	1. 2. 3. 4.				
Text Work	1. 2. 3. 4.				
Character/ Style Study	1. 2. 3. 4.				
Listening	1. 2. 3. 4.				
Totals					

May 3, 2019	Friday	Saturday	Sunday	Totals	Questions
Warm-ups and exercises					
Repertoire					
Text Work					
Character/ Style Study					
Listening					

May 6, 2019	Assignments for this week	Monday	Tuesday	Wednesday	Thursday
Warm-ups and exercises	1. 2. 3. 4.				
Repertoire	1. 2. 3. 4.				
Text Work	1. 2. 3. 4.				
Character/ Style Study	1. 2. 3. 4.				
Listening	1. 2. 3. 4.				
Totals					

May 10, 2019	Friday	Saturday	Sunday	Totals	Questions
Warm-ups and exercises					
Repertoire					
Text Work					
Character/ Style Study					
Listening					

Month to date total:_____   40   Year to date total_____

May 13, 2019	Assignments for this week	Monday	Tuesday	Wednesday	Thursday
Warm-ups and exercises	1. 2. 3. 4.				
Repertoire	1. 2. 3. 4.				
Text Work	1. 2. 3. 4.				
Character/ Style Study	1. 2. 3. 4.				
Listening	1. 2. 3. 4.				
Totals					

May 17, 2019	Friday	Saturday	Sunday	Totals	Questions
Warm-ups and exercises					
Repertoire					
Text Work					
Character/ Style Study					
Listening					

May 20, 2019	Assignments for this week	Monday	Tuesday	Wednesday	Thursday
Warm-ups and exercises	1. 2. 3. 4.				
Repertoire	1. 2. 3. 4.				
Text Work	1. 2. 3. 4.				
Character/ Style Study	1. 2. 3. 4.				
Listening	1. 2. 3. 4.				
Totals					

May 24, 2019	Friday	Saturday	Sunday	Totals	Questions
Warm-ups and exercises					
Repertoire					
Text Work					
Character/ Style Study					
Listening					

May 27, 2019	Assignments for this week	Monday	Tuesday	Wednesday	Thursday
Warm-ups and exercises	1. 2. 3. 4.				
Repertoire	1. 2. 3. 4.				
Text Work	1. 2. 3. 4.				
Character/ Style Study	1. 2. 3. 4.				
Listening	1. 2. 3. 4.				
Totals					

May 31, 2019	Friday	Saturday	Sunday	Totals	Questions
Warm-ups and exercises					
Repertoire					
Text Work					
Character/ Style Study					
Listening					

Month to date total:_____

Year to date total_____

June 3, 2019	Assignments for this week	Monday	Tuesday	Wednesday	Thursday
Warm-ups and exercises	1. 2. 3. 4.				
Repertoire	1. 2. 3. 4.				
Text Work	1. 2. 3. 4.				
Character/ Style Study	1. 2. 3. 4.				
Listening	1. 2. 3. 4.				
Totals					

June 7, 2019	Friday	Saturday	Sunday	Totals	Questions
Warm-ups and exercises					
Repertoire					
Text Work					
Character/ Style Study					
Listening					

June 10, 2019	Assignments for this week	Monday	Tuesday	Wednesday	Thursday
Warm-ups and exercises	1. 2. 3. 4.				
Repertoire	1. 2. 3. 4.				
Text Work	1. 2. 3. 4.				
Character/ Style Study	1. 2. 3. 4.				
Listening	1. 2. 3. 4.				
Totals					

June 14, 2019	Friday	Saturday	Sunday	Totals	Questions
Warm-ups and exercises					
Repertoire					
Text Work					
Character/ Style Study					
Listening					

June 17, 2019	Assignments for this week	Monday	Tuesday	Wednesday	Thursday
Warm-ups and exercises	1. 2. 3. 4.				
Repertoire	1. 2. 3. 4.				
Text Work	1. 2. 3. 4.				
Character/ Style Study	1. 2. 3. 4.				
Listening	1. 2. 3. 4.				
Totals					

June 21, 2019	Friday	Saturday	Sunday	Totals	Questions
Warm-ups and exercises					
Repertoire					
Text Work					
Character/ Style Study					
Listening					

Month to date total:_____

Year to date total_____

June 24, 2019	Assignments for this week	Monday	Tuesday	Wednesday	Thursday
Warm-ups and exercises	1. 2. 3. 4.				
Repertoire	1. 2. 3. 4.				
Text Work	1. 2. 3. 4.				
Character/ Style Study	1. 2. 3. 4.				
Listening	1. 2. 3. 4.				
Totals					

June 28, 2019	Friday	Saturday	Sunday	Totals	Questions
Warm-ups and exercises					
Repertoire					
Text Work					
Character/ Style Study					
Listening					

July 1, 2019	Assignments for this week	Monday	Tuesday	Wednesday	Thursday
Warm-ups and exercises	1. 2. 3. 4.				
Repertoire	1. 2. 3. 4.				
Text Work	1. 2. 3. 4.				
Character/ Style Study	1. 2. 3. 4.				
Listening	1. 2. 3. 4.				
Totals					

July 5, 2019	Friday	Saturday	Sunday	Totals	Questions
Warm-ups and exercises					
Repertoire					
Text Work					
Character/ Style Study					
Listening					

July 8, 2019	Assignments for this week	Monday	Tuesday	Wednesday	Thursday
Warm-ups and exercises	1. 2. 3. 4.				
Repertoire	1. 2. 3. 4.				
Text Work	1. 2. 3. 4.				
Character/ Style Study	1. 2. 3. 4.				
Listening	1. 2. 3. 4.				
Totals					

July 12, 2019	Friday	Saturday	Sunday	Totals	Questions
Warm-ups and exercises					
Repertoire					
Text Work					
Character/ Style Study					
Listening					

July 15, 2019	Assignments for this week	Monday	Tuesday	Wednesday	Thursday
Warm-ups and exercises	1. 2. 3. 4.				
Repertoire	1. 2. 3. 4.				
Text Work	1. 2. 3. 4.				
Character/ Style Study	1. 2. 3. 4.				
Listening	1. 2. 3. 4.				
Totals					

Month to date total:_____

Year to date total_____

July 19, 2019	Friday	Saturday	Sunday	Totals	Questions
Warm-ups and exercises					
Repertoire					
Text Work					
Character/ Style Study					
Listening					

July 22, 2019	Assignments for this week	Monday	Tuesday	Wednesday	Thursday
Warm-ups and exercises	1. 2. 3. 4.				
Repertoire	1. 2. 3. 4.				
Text Work	1. 2. 3. 4.				
Character/ Style Study	1. 2. 3. 4.				
Listening	1. 2. 3. 4.				
Totals					

July 26, 2019	Friday	Saturday	Sunday	Totals	Questions
Warm-ups and exercises					
Repertoire					
Text Work					
Character/ Style Study					
Listening					

July 29, 2019	Assignments for this week	Monday	Tuesday	Wednesday	Thursday
Warm-ups and exercises	1. 2. 3. 4.				
Repertoire	1. 2. 3. 4.				
Text Work	1. 2. 3. 4.				
Character/ Style Study	1. 2. 3. 4.				
Listening	1. 2. 3. 4.				
Totals					

Month to date total:_____

63

Year to date total_____

August 2, 2019	Friday	Saturday	Sunday	Totals	Questions
Warm-ups and exercises					
Repertoire					
Text Work					
Character/ Style Study					
Listening					

August 5, 2019	Assignments for this week	Monday	Tuesday	Wednesday	Thursday
Warm-ups and exercises	1. 2. 3. 4.				
Repertoire	1. 2. 3. 4.				
Text Work	1. 2. 3. 4.				
Character/ Style Study	1. 2. 3. 4.				
Listening	1. 2. 3. 4.				
Totals					

August 9, 2019	Friday	Saturday	Sunday	Totals	Questions
Warm-ups and exercises					
Repertoire					
Text Work					
Character/ Style Study					
Listening					

Month to date total:_____

Year to date total_____

August 12, 2019	Assignments for this week	Monday	Tuesday	Wednesday	Thursday
Warm-ups and exercises	1. 2. 3. 4.				
Repertoire	1. 2. 3. 4.				
Text Work	1. 2. 3. 4.				
Character/ Style Study	1. 2. 3. 4.				
Listening	1. 2. 3. 4.				
Totals					

August 16, 2019	Friday	Saturday	Sunday	Totals	Questions
Warm-ups and exercises					
Repertoire					
Text Work					
Character/ Style Study					
Listening					

August 19, 2019	Assignments for this week	Monday	Tuesday	Wednesday	Thursday
Warm-ups and exercises	1. 2. 3. 4.				
Repertoire	1. 2. 3. 4.				
Text Work	1. 2. 3. 4.				
Character/ Style Study	1. 2. 3. 4.				
Listening	1. 2. 3. 4.				
Totals					

August 23, 2019	Friday	Saturday	Sunday	Totals	Questions
Warm-ups and exercises					
Repertoire					
Text Work					
Character/ Style Study					
Listening					

August 26, 2019	Assignments for this week	Monday	Tuesday	Wednesday	Thursday
Warm-ups and exercises	1. 2. 3. 4.				
Repertoire	1. 2. 3. 4.				
Text Work	1. 2. 3. 4.				
Character/ Style Study	1. 2. 3. 4.				
Listening	1. 2. 3. 4.				
Totals					

August 30, 2019	Friday	Saturday	Sunday	Totals	Questions
Warm-ups and exercises					
Repertoire					
Text Work					
Character/ Style Study					
Listening					

September 2, 2019	Assignments for this week	Monday	Tuesday	Wednesday	Thursday
Warm-ups and exercises	1. 2. 3. 4.				
Repertoire	1. 2. 3. 4.				
Text Work	1. 2. 3. 4.				
Character/ Style Study	1. 2. 3. 4.				
Listening	1. 2. 3. 4.				
Totals					

September 6, 2019	Friday	Saturday	Sunday	Totals	Questions
Warm-ups and exercises					
Repertoire					
Text Work					
Character/ Style Study					
Listening					

September 9, 2019	Assignments for this week	Monday	Tuesday	Wednesday	Thursday
Warm-ups and exercises	1. 2. 3. 4.				
Repertoire	1. 2. 3. 4.				
Text Work	1. 2. 3. 4.				
Character/ Style Study	1. 2. 3. 4.				
Listening	1. 2. 3. 4.				
Totals					

September 13, 2019	Friday	Saturday	Sunday	Totals	Questions
Warm-ups and exercises					
Repertoire					
Text Work					
Character/ Style Study					
Listening					

September 16, 2019	Assignments for this week	Monday	Tuesday	Wednesday	Thursday
Warm-ups and exercises	1. 2. 3. 4.				
Repertoire	1. 2. 3. 4.				
Text Work	1. 2. 3. 4.				
Character/ Style Study	1. 2. 3. 4.				
Listening	1. 2. 3. 4.				
Totals					

September 20, 2019	Friday	Saturday	Sunday	Totals	Questions
Warm-ups and exercises					
Repertoire					
Text Work					
Character/ Style Study					
Listening					

September 23, 2019	Assignments for this week	Monday	Tuesday	Wednesday	Thursday
Warm-ups and exercises	1. 2. 3. 4.				
Repertoire	1. 2. 3. 4.				
Text Work	1. 2. 3. 4.				
Character/ Style Study	1. 2. 3. 4.				
Listening	1. 2. 3. 4.				
Totals					

Month to date total:_____

Year to date total_____

September 27, 2019	Friday	Saturday	Sunday	Totals	Questions
Warm-ups and exercises					
Repertoire					
Text Work					
Character/ Style Study					
Listening					

September 30, 2019	Assignments for this week	Monday	Tuesday	Wednesday	Thursday
Warm-ups and exercises	1. 2. 3. 4.				
Repertoire	1. 2. 3. 4.				
Text Work	1. 2. 3. 4.				
Character/ Style Study	1. 2. 3. 4.				
Listening	1. 2. 3. 4.				
Totals					

Month to date total:_____

Year to date total_____

October 4, 2019	Friday	Saturday	Sunday	Totals	Questions
Warm-ups and exercises					
Repertoire					
Text Work					
Character/ Style Study					
Listening					

October 7, 2019	Assignments for this week	Monday	Tuesday	Wednesday	Thursday
Warm-ups and exercises	1. 2. 3. 4.				
Repertoire	1. 2. 3. 4.				
Text Work	1. 2. 3. 4.				
Character/ Style Study	1. 2. 3. 4.				
Listening	1. 2. 3. 4.				
Totals					

October 11, 2019	Friday	Saturday	Sunday	Totals	Questions
Warm-ups and exercises					
Repertoire					
Text Work					
Character/ Style Study					
Listening					

Month to date total:_____

Year to date total_____

October 14, 2019	Assignments for this week	Monday	Tuesday	Wednesday	Thursday
Warm-ups and exercises	1. 2. 3. 4.				
Repertoire	1. 2. 3. 4.				
Text Work	1. 2. 3. 4.				
Character/ Style Study	1. 2. 3. 4.				
Listening	1. 2. 3. 4.				
Totals					

October 18, 2019	Friday	Saturday	Sunday	Totals	Questions
Warm-ups and exercises					
Repertoire					
Text Work					
Character/ Style Study					
Listening					

October 21, 2019	Assignments for this week	Monday	Tuesday	Wednesday	Thursday
Warm-ups and exercises	1. 2. 3. 4.				
Repertoire	1. 2. 3. 4.				
Text Work	1. 2. 3. 4.				
Character/ Style Study	1. 2. 3. 4.				
Listening	1. 2. 3. 4.				
Totals					

Month to date total:_____

Year to date total_____

October 25, 2019	Friday	Saturday	Sunday	Totals	Questions
Warm-ups and exercises					
Repertoire					
Text Work					
Character/ Style Study					
Listening					

October 28, 2019	Assignments for this week	Monday	Tuesday	Wednesday	Thursday
Warm-ups and exercises	1. 2. 3. 4.				
Repertoire	1. 2. 3. 4.				
Text Work	1. 2. 3. 4.				
Character/ Style Study	1. 2. 3. 4.				
Listening	1. 2. 3. 4.				
Totals					

November 1, 2019	Friday	Saturday	Sunday	Totals	Questions
Warm-ups and exercises					
Repertoire					
Text Work					
Character/ Style Study					
Listening					

November 4, 2019	Assignments for this week	Monday	Tuesday	Wednesday	Thursday
Warm-ups and exercises	1. 2. 3. 4.				
Repertoire	1. 2. 3. 4.				
Text Work	1. 2. 3. 4.				
Character/ Style Study	1. 2. 3. 4.				
Listening	1. 2. 3. 4.				
Totals					

November 8, 2019	Friday	Saturday	Sunday	Totals	Questions
Warm-ups and exercises					
Repertoire					
Text Work					
Character/ Style Study					
Listening					

Month to date total:_____

Year to date total_____

November 11, 2019	Assignments for this week	Monday	Tuesday	Wednesday	Thursday
Warm-ups and exercises	1. 2. 3. 4.				
Repertoire	1. 2. 3. 4.				
Text Work	1. 2. 3. 4.				
Character/ Style Study	1. 2. 3. 4.				
Listening	1. 2. 3. 4.				
Totals					

November 15, 2019	Friday	Saturday	Sunday	Totals	Questions
Warm-ups and exercises					
Repertoire					
Text Work					
Character/ Style Study					
Listening					

November 18, 2019	Assignments for this week	Monday	Tuesday	Wednesday	Thursday
Warm-ups and exercises	1. 2. 3. 4.				
Repertoire	1. 2. 3. 4.				
Text Work	1. 2. 3. 4.				
Character/ Style Study	1. 2. 3. 4.				
Listening	1. 2. 3. 4.				
Totals					

November 22, 2019	Friday	Saturday	Sunday	Totals	Questions
Warm-ups and exercises					
Repertoire					
Text Work					
Character/ Style Study					
Listening					

November 25, 2019	Assignments for this week	Monday	Tuesday	Wednesday	Thursday
Warm-ups and exercises	1. 2. 3. 4.				
Repertoire	1. 2. 3. 4.				
Text Work	1. 2. 3. 4.				
Character/ Style Study	1. 2. 3. 4.				
Listening	1. 2. 3. 4.				
Totals					

November 29, 2019	Friday	Saturday	Sunday	Totals	Questions
Warm-ups and exercises					
Repertoire					
Text Work					
Character/ Style Study					
Listening					

December 2, 2019	Assignments for this week	Monday	Tuesday	Wednesday	Thursday
Warm-ups and exercises	1. 2. 3. 4.				
Repertoire	1. 2. 3. 4.				
Text Work	1. 2. 3. 4.				
Character/ Style Study	1. 2. 3. 4.				
Listening	1. 2. 3. 4.				
Totals					

December 6, 2019	Friday	Saturday	Sunday	Totals	Questions
Warm-ups and exercises					
Repertoire					
Text Work					
Character/ Style Study					
Listening					

December 9, 2019	Assignments for this week	Monday	Tuesday	Wednesday	Thursday
Warm-ups and exercises	1. 2. 3. 4.				
Repertoire	1. 2. 3. 4.				
Text Work	1. 2. 3. 4.				
Character/ Style Study	1. 2. 3. 4.				
Listening	1. 2. 3. 4.				
Totals					

December 13, 2019	Friday	Saturday	Sunday	Totals	Questions
Warm-ups and exercises					
Repertoire					
Text Work					
Character/ Style Study					
Listening					

December 16, 2019	Assignments for this week	Monday	Tuesday	Wednesday	Thursday
Warm-ups and exercises	1. 2. 3. 4.				
Repertoire	1. 2. 3. 4.				
Text Work	1. 2. 3. 4.				
Character/ Style Study	1. 2. 3. 4.				
Listening	1. 2. 3. 4.				
Totals					

December 20, 2019	Friday	Saturday	Sunday	Totals	Questions
Warm-ups and exercises					
Repertoire					
Text Work					
Character/ Style Study					
Listening					

December 23, 2019	Assignments for this week	Monday	Tuesday	Wednesday	Thursday
Warm-ups and exercises	1. 2. 3. 4.				
Repertoire	1. 2. 3. 4.				
Text Work	1. 2. 3. 4.				
Character/ Style Study	1. 2. 3. 4.				
Listening	1. 2. 3. 4.				
Totals					

December 27, 2019	Friday	Saturday	Sunday	Totals	Questions
Warm-ups and exercises					
Repertoire					
Text Work					
Character/ Style Study					
Listening					

Month to date total:_____   Year to date total_____

December 30, 2019	Assignments for this week	Monday	Tuesday	Wednesday	Thursday
Warm-ups and exercises	1. 2. 3. 4.				
Repertoire	1. 2. 3. 4.				
Text Work	1. 2. 3. 4.				
Character/ Style Study	1. 2. 3. 4.				
Listening	1. 2. 3. 4.				
Totals					

January 3, 2020	Friday	Saturday	Sunday	Totals	Questions
Warm-ups and exercises					
Repertoire					
Text Work					
Character/ Style Study					
Listening					

Month to date total:_____

Year to date total_____

www.ingramcontent.com/pod-product-compliance
Lightning Source LLC
Chambersburg PA
CBHW081155180526

45170CB00006B/2085